WORKBOOK

AQA A-LEVEL

Economics 2

TOPICS 9–14

The national and international economy

David Horner and
Steve Stoddard

Orders: please contact Bookpoint Ltd, 130 Park Drive, Milton Park, Abingdon, Oxon OX14 4SE. Telephone: +44 (0)1235 827827. Fax: +44 (0)1235 400401. Email education@bookpoint. co.uk Lines are open from 9 a.m. to 5 p.m., Monday to Saturday, with a 24-hour message answering service. You can also order through our website: www.hoddereducation.co.uk

ISBN: 978 1 5104 8324 8

© David Horner and Steve Stoddard 2020

First published in 2020 by
Hodder Education,
An Hachette UK Company
Carmelite House
50 Victoria Embankment

London EC4Y 0DZ

www.hoddereducation.co.uk

Impression number   10 9 8 7 6 5 4 3 2 1

Year   2024 2023 2022 2021 2020

Cover photo © vadim.nefedov – stock.adobe.com

Typeset in Integra Software Services Pvt. Ltd., Pondicherry.

Printed in India

A catalogue record for this title is available from the British Library.

Contents

About this book

1 **This workbook** will help you to prepare for AQA A-level Economics Topics 9–14.

2 **Topics 9–14** could be assessed in:
- A-level Paper 2, which lasts for 2 hours and covers Topics 9–14. Paper 2 is worth 33.3% of the A-level. Section A requires you to choose one data response context from a choice of two, followed by questions worth 2, 4, 9 and 25 marks. Section B requires you to choose one essay from a choice of three, with the first part of each essay worth 15 marks and the second part worth 25 marks.
- A-level Paper 3, which lasts for 2 hours and covers Topics 1–14. Paper 3 is also worth 33.3% of the A-level. Section A has 30 multi-choice questions, worth 30 marks in total. Section B is based upon a series of numerical and written extracts followed by questions worth 10, 15 and 25 marks. All questions are compulsory.

3 For each topic in this workbook there are:
- stimulus materials, including key terms and concepts
- short-answer questions that build up to exam-style questions
- spaces for you to write or plan your answers
- questions that test your mathematical skills

4 **Answering the questions** will help you to build your skills and meet the assessment objectives AO1 (knowledge and understanding), AO2 (application), AO3 (analysis) and AO4 (evaluation). Quantitative skills will make up a minimum of 20% of the total marks across the A-level.

5 **Worked answers** are included throughout the practice questions to help you understand how to gain the most marks.

6 Icons next to the question will help you to identify:

where your calculations skills are tested

where questions draw on synoptic knowledge, i.e. content from more than one topic

how long this question should take you

7 **You still need** to read your textbook and refer to your revision guides and lesson notes.

8 **Marks available** are indicated for all questions so that you can gauge the level of detail required in your answers.

9 **Timings** are given for the exam-style questions to make your practice as realistic as possible.

10 Answers are available at: www.hoddereducation.co.uk/workbookanswers.

Topic 9 The measurement of macroeconomic performance

The objectives of government economic policy

Economic performance is measured by achievement of the government's objectives for the economy. These objectives represent goals to be achieved. The main priorities of these objectives include low unemployment, stable (and low) inflation, positive and sustainable economic growth, and a balance on the current account of the balance of payments.

There are also potential policy conflicts, where achieving one objective means moving away from achieving other objectives. Some disagree that these conflicts exist.

Practice questions ?

AO1: Knowledge and understanding

1 Define the term 'unemployment'.   3 marks

Worked example

Unemployment refers to those from the population of working age who are currently without a job but are actively seeking work.

AO1: This answer covers the three main aspects of the definition: population of working age; currently without a job; actively seeking work. It therefore scores full marks.

2 Distinguish between the terms 'microeconomics' and 'macroeconomics'.   2 marks

....

....

3 Define the term 'economic growth'.   3 marks

....

....

4 Distinguish between macroeconomic objectives and macroeconomic policies.   3 marks

....

....

....

5 Explain why a fall in economic growth does not necessarily mean a fall in national income.   3 marks

....

....

....

6   Which of the following would be used to calculate the current account balance?   *2 marks*

    a   government revenue from taxation of foreign trade

    b   exports of services

    c   government expenditure on UK industry

    d   imports of raw materials

....

....

7   Explain why income inequality may fall even if the richest 10% of households see their incomes rise over time.   *3 marks*

....

....

....

AO2: Application

8   If GDP was £4,865.60 billion in 2019, and the economy grew by 1.6% between 2019 and 2020, calculate the level of GDP for 2020.   *2 marks*

....

....

9   Economic growth in an economy was 2.1%. GDP at the start of the year was measured at £22,378,900 million. Calculate the value of GDP at the end of the current year.   *2 marks*

....

....

10   GDP in 2018 was £1,087,500 million. By 2019 GDP had risen to £1,115,529 million. Calculate economic growth for 2018–19 to one decimal place.   *2 marks*

....

....

11   The following table relates to the output of an economy and the number of people in employment.

Year	Output (units)	Number in employment
1	145,600	2,000
2	148,400	2,120

Calculate the productivity per worker for both years.   *2 marks*

....

....

Macroeconomic indicators and index numbers

Economic objectives are measured through a number of official indicators. Macroeconomic indicators include real gross domestic product (GDP), real GDP per capita, the inflation rate, the unemployment rate, the budget balance as well as the balance on the current account of the balance of payments. All of these are expressed in numerical form — as values or rates. Index numbers can be used to make it easier to monitor changes in these indicators.

Practice questions ?

AO1: Knowledge and understanding

12 State the two measures of unemployment used in the UK.　　　　2 marks

....

....

13 Distinguish between real and nominal GDP.　　　　3 marks

....

....

....

14 Define the term 'GDP per capita'.　　　　3 marks

....

....

15 Explain what is meant by the term 'price level'.　　　　2 marks

....

....

16 Fill in the missing economic indicators in the following table.　　　　4 marks

Description	Economic indicator
a National income adjusted for price changes	
b Average real national income	
c Measure of price increases over 1 year	
d Value of exports exceeds value of imports	

17 Explain what is meant by a 'weighted basket of goods' as used in the CPI calculation.　　　　3 marks

....

....

....

18 The table below shows details for a weighted price index that contains three products: A, B and C.

Product	Year 1 price (£)	Year 2 price (£)	Weight
A	5	8	2
B	20	22	4
C	25	20	1

If year 1 is the base year, what is the value of the weighted price index in year 2?   *4 marks*

Worked example

Based on the year 2 prices, the year 2 price index: A 160, B 110, C 80

Year 2 weighted price index: A 320, B 440, C 80

Total of weights divided by weights = 840/7 = 120. Price index in year 2 = 120

A01: There is a correct use of data, with correct calculations for the year 2 index numbers. These are then 'weighted', apparently with a final calculation of the price index in full for year 2. **A02:** Full workings are shown and carried out methodically, gaining full marks.

19 Based on the following data, calculate the GDP per capita for 2020.   *2 marks*

GDP in 2019	$640 billion
Economic growth (2019–20)	4%
Population in 2020	25 million

....

....

20 At December 2018, the CPI was 224.5. By December 2019, the CPI had risen to 228.4. Calculate the inflation rate for the year to December 2019.   *2 marks*

....

....

21 The following table contains the price index for an economy between 2016 and 2020. What was the highest and lowest inflation rate over this period?   *4 marks*

Year	Price index
2016	100
2017	105
2018	108
2019	112
2020	117

....

....

....

AO3: Analysis

22 Explain two reasons why the labour force survey and the claimant count measures of unemployment give different results. 4 marks

....

....

....

....

23 Analyse two limitations of the CPI as a measure of inflation used in the UK. 6 marks

....

....

....

....

24 Analyse two benefits of using index numbers compared with using actual numbers when analysing economic data. 6 marks

....

....

....

....

....

Uses of national income data

Gross domestic product (GDP) represents national income for the economy. GDP can be useful in representing the standard of living enjoyed by an economy's population, though this approach does have limitations. When making GDP comparisons between countries, an appropriate exchange rate should be used, and the concept of purchasing power parity (PPP) is useful in making comparisons more meaningful.

Practice questions ?

AO1: Knowledge and understanding

25 State three uses of national income. 3 marks

....

....

....

26 State three adjustments that could be made to nominal GDP to make it a more accurate indicator of living standards. **3 marks**

....

....

....

27 State three non-financial factors that contribute to the standard of living. **3 marks**

....

....

....

28 Explain the term 'purchasing power parity'. **3 marks**

....

....

....

29 Explain what is meant by the term 'non-marketed output'. **3 marks**

....

....

....

30 Explain what is meant by the 'shadow economy'. **3 marks**

....

....

....

AO2: Application

31 Explain why the composition of GDP matters when assessing living standards. **3 marks**

....

....

....

32 Using knowledge of purchasing power parity (PPP), explain what happens to the exchange rate if prices are higher in one country compared with another. **3 marks**

....

....

33 Based on the following information about price indices, what would you expect the (£/$) exchange rate to be if PPP alone can explain exchange rate movements?　2 marks

Price index in USA	180
Price index in UK	120

....

....

34 Price index data for two countries appear below. The exchange rate is currently £1 = $1.95. Explain what you think would happen to the exchange rate in country 1 based on PPP theory.　4 marks

Country	Price index
Country 1 (uses £)	242
Country 2 (uses $)	395

....

....

....

....

AO3: Analysis

35 Analyse two reasons why real GDP does not reflect living standards in an economy.　8 marks

The worked example below shows a model paragraph from a possible response to this question, explaining one reason why real GDP does not reflect living standards. Study this closely and then attempt to provide a full answer to the question on a separate piece of paper.

Worked example

One reason why real GDP does not reflect living standards is that it does not take into account inequality in the distribution of income. Per capita GDP shows an average amount of income for the population but this is not representative of most people's incomes. Incomes vary and this means many people have an income either above or below this average level, and their living standards may be significantly different from those of people on average incomes. The greater the level of inequality, the less likely it is that the average income reflects the living standards of many of the population. This could mean that although the average income is high, it may only be high due to a small number of very high earners pulling up the average, i.e. most do not enjoy the income level that the average level would suggest.

AO1: Valid reason is identified — that incomes are not evenly distributed.

AO2: Explanation of why this means per capita income does not always reflect living standards is applied to the question and correctly developed.

AO3: Analysis is included here by developing how the level of inequality may make per capita income less reliable — depending on how unequally income is distributed.

36 Explain two uses of national income. **6 marks**

....

....

....

....

....

37 Explain two non-income factors that affect the standard of living for individuals. **4 marks**

....

....

....

....

38 Explain how the production of negative externalities can both add to and subtract from an individual's quality of life. **4 marks**

....

....

....

....

39 Explain one limitation of PPP as a theory of exchange rate determination. **3 marks**

....

....

....

40 A large welfare state financed by high taxes may mean that GDP per capita is less effective at reflecting living standards. Explain why this is the case. **3 marks**

....

....

....

AO4: Evaluation

Write your answers to these questions on separate sheets of paper and keep them with your workbook.

41 To what extent does using PPP data make GDP per capita a reliable measure of living standards? **25 marks**

42 Evaluate the extent to which we need to consider the composition of GDP rather than the level of GDP when measuring the welfare enjoyed by the population of any economy.

25 marks

Topic 9: Multiple choice and short answer

1 Which of the following is a macroeconomic objective of the UK government?

A low inflation

B low economic growth

C high unemployment

D high deficit on the current account

54

2 The following table shows the prices of two goods (X and Y) over a 4-year period. The base year is year 2.

Year	Good X	Good Y
Year 1	75	80
Year 2	100	100
Year 3	120	125
Year 4	130	130

Based on these data, which of the following statements can be said to be true?

A Good Y started off the period at a higher price than Good X.

B The price of Good X rose by a larger percentage over the whole period covered.

C Good Y had the biggest year-on-year price rise measured as a percentage increase.

D In real terms, the price of Good Y rose by the least.

3 Which of the following is not normally considered to be a useful indicator of economic performance?

A balance of payments on current account

B index numbers

C changes in the consumer price index

D levels of claimant count unemployment

4 The table below includes the output level and employment level for an economy for a 2-year period.

Year	Output level	Number in employment
Year 1	125	95
Year 2	132	102

From the table, which of the following cannot be concluded?

A Output levels rose.

B Employment levels rose.

C Productivity increased.

D Productivity decreased.

5   Which of the following best describes the use of PPP exchange rates when comparing living standards between countries?

   A   Rising prices will mean that national income may not reflect the actual purchasing power of the population.

   B   Converting national incomes into common exchange rates may be misleading if exchange rates are volatile.

   C   National income per capita may be misleading if income distribution is very unequal.

   D   Provision of welfare benefits and progressive taxes make comparisons of living standards less valid.

6   GDP rose from £890 billion to £915 billion over a 1-year period. Calculate the level of economic growth for this period.   **2 marks**

   ....

   ....

7   In an economy at the end of the year, GDP was measured at $4,943.45 billion. If economic growth in the most recent year had been 1.6%, what was the value of GDP at the start of the current year?   **2 marks**

   ....

   ....

8   Do the data shown in the following table support the view that living standards in this country have improved over time?   **4 marks**

Year	Real GDP per capita
2016	$36,780
2017	$39,805
2018	$39,334
2019	$40,908
2020	$41,100

   ....

   ....

   ....

   ....

9   Analyse the usefulness of GDP data for a government making economic decisions.   **9 marks**

   ....

   ....

   ....

   ....

   ....

   ....

   ....

   ....

10 Analyse why GDP per capita does not accurately reflect the population's living standards.

15 marks

....

....

....

....

....

....

....

....

....

....

....

....

....

....

....

....

....

....

....

....

....

.... Analyse why GDP per capita does not accurately reflect the population's living standards. ....

Topic 9: Data response

11 Read Extracts A and B and answer the following questions.   **40 marks**

Extract A

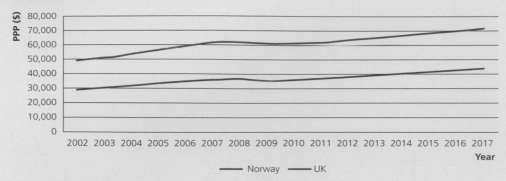

(60)

Real GDP per capita 2002–17, measured in US dollars ($)

Extract B

According to the UN, Norway is the best country in the world to live in. The 2018 results once again place Norway as the country with the highest score on the human development index (HDI). It has maintained first place in the HDI rankings now for a number of years, despite only coming in sixth place in terms of income per head (Norway's GDP per capita is estimated at $75,000 per person).

Unlike GDP, which measures the income of an economy, the HDI attempts to give a wider view of the population's wellbeing by including income per person, health and education factors within its calculation. Other countries scoring highly on the HDI measure are Australia, Switzerland, Denmark and Norway.

The UK comes 14th in the HDI ranking, which is higher than the ranking it receives if GDP per capita alone is used to rank countries.

Some have argued that GDP per capita is a crude measure of the population's quality of life anyway and that it is a highly flawed statistic. Attempts to come up with a better measurement of quality of life or living standards have so far been unsuccessful, however, and GDP per capita remains the single most used statistic in determining the population's wellbeing.

a If the population of Norway is 5.3 million, then using Extract B, calculate the overall level of GDP for Norway in US$ for 2018.   **2 marks**

....

....

b Do the data used in Extract A support the view that living standards in the UK have risen since 2002?   **4 marks**

....

....

....

....

c   Analyse why most governments have economic growth as one of their
economic objectives.   **9 marks**

....

....

....

....

....

....

d   To what extent is HDI a better indicator of the standard of living of the
population of a country than its GDP per capita?   **25 marks**

*Write your answer to this question on a separate sheet of paper and keep it
with your workbook.*

Exam-style questions ?

Topic 9: Essay

12 Analyse the determinants of a population's standard of living.   **15 marks** 60

....

....

....

....

....

....

....

....

....

....

....

13 Evaluate the extent to which living standards are determined by changes
in income.   **25 marks**

*Write your answer to this question on a separate sheet of paper and keep it with
your workbook.*

Topic 10 How the macroeconomy works

National income and the circular flow of income

The level of national income — normally measured by GDP — can be found by using economic models, which are representations of how the economy actually works. One model used is the circular flow of income. This model shows us how real national income is determined and how rises or falls in real national income depend on the actions of households and businesses. A more complex model of the circular flow also shows how the government and foreign trade sectors influence the level of GDP.

Practice questions ?

AO1: Knowledge and understanding

1   Define the term 'macroeconomic equilibrium'.   3 marks

> **Worked example**
>
> Macroeconomic equilibrium occurs when there is no tendency for the price level or level of national income to change. This will occur where injections equal leakages, or *AD* equals *AS*.

AO1: This answer covers the key aspects of the definition, supported with a relevant application of equilibrium to an economic model (*AD/AS*).

2   State the three methods of calculating national income.   3 marks

....

....

....

3   Complete the following table by inserting the three injections and three withdrawals into the circular flow of income.   3 marks

Injections	Withdrawals

4   Explain the term 'circular flow of income'.   3 marks

....

....

5   Define the term 'real national income'.   3 marks

....

....

6   In the context of national income accounts, explain what is meant by double-counting.   3 marks

....

....

7 Explain what is meant by consumption.

3 marks

....

....

AO2: Application

8 Based on the following data, calculate the rate of real economic growth between 2019 and 2020.

4 marks

Year	Nominal GDP ($ billions)	Price level
2019	9,950	100
2020	10,680	104

Worked example

Real GDP in 2020 = nominal GDP in 2020 × (price level in 2019/price level in 2020)

$$= \$10,680bn \times (100/104) = \$10,269.2bn$$

Real economic growth in 2020 = percentage change in real GDP between 2019 and 2020

$$= (\$10,269.2bn - \$9,950bn)/\$9,950bn \times 100$$

$$= 3.2\%$$

AO2: The correct steps are taken — first the calculation of real GDP for 2020, to allow the calculation of real growth in the second step — with appropriate workings shown.

9 Based on the following data, calculate the rate of real economic growth over the 10-year period.

4 marks

Year	Nominal GDP (£ millions)	Price level
2010	113,888	154
2020	164,410	181

....

....

....

10 The following data relate to the circular flow of income in an economy. Using appropriate calculations, decide what will happen to the level of national income in this economy.

3 marks

	£ millions
Investment	480
Government expenditure	310
Exports	190
Saving	370
Taxation	330
Imports	360

....

....

....

....

....

....

....

11 Assuming the economy is in equilibrium in each scenario, complete the following table.

4 marks

Scenario	Savings (£m)	Government spending (£m)	Imports (£m)	Exports (£m)	Taxation (£m)	Investment (£m)
Scenario 1	5,277		1,101	1,048	4,878	6,010
Scenario 2	14,151	13,131		10,190	7,675	8,496
Scenario 3	8,797	8,445	10,012	8,610		11,067
Scenario 4		13,445	8,762	14,215	17,313	19,805

AO3: Analysis

12 Explain how an increase in injections into the circular flow affects the level of national income.

4 marks

....

....

....

....

13 Explain why an economy can be in equilibrium despite it having both a budget deficit and a trade deficit at the same time.

4 marks

....

....

....

....

14 Explain why when the economy is in equilibrium, total output will be equal to both total income and total expenditure.

4 marks

....

....

....

....

Determinants of aggregate demand and the multiplier

Another economic model is that of aggregate demand (*AD*) and aggregate supply (*AS*). *AD* represents the total planned spending of the different major economic agents — the household, the business, the government and the foreign trade sectors of the economy. Changes in planned spending can significantly affect overall economic performance.

Changes in the level of *AD* are also affected by the workings of the economic multiplier, which can magnify both increases and decreases in spending.

Practice questions **?**

AO1: Knowledge and understanding

15 State the four components of aggregate demand (*AD*). 4 marks

....

....

....

....

16 Explain one reason why the *AD* curve slopes downwards. 3 marks

....

....

....

17 Explain the term 'negative multiplier'. 3 marks

....

....

....

18 Define the term 'wealth effect'. 3 marks

....

....

....

19 Define the term 'accelerator theory'. 3 marks

....

....

....

20 State which of the following would be a movement along the *AD* curve and which would lead to a shift in the *AD* curve:

a   a rise in the price level

b   a decrease in direct tax rates

c   an increase in wage rates

d   increased consumer pessimism

e   a fall in interest rates   5 marks

....

....

21 Decide which of the following would shift the *AD* curve to the left or to the right (ignoring any potential effects on *AS*):

a   a rise in government spending

b   a rise in both house and share prices

c   a rise in interest rates

d   a rise in the exchange rate

e   a rise in corporation tax rates   5 marks

....

....

AO2: Application

22 In an economy, the following information is available.

- Consumption is £2,200,000 million, of which 25% is spent on imported goods and services.

- Government expenditure is £975,000 million.

- Investment is £475,000 million.

- There is a trade deficit of £83,600 million.

Based on this information, calculate the level of *AD*.   4 marks

....

....

....

23 The multiplier is estimated to be 1.8. If national income rises by £360 million, calculate the size of the initial change in *AD*.   2 marks

....

....

24 For each of the following *MPC*s, calculate the size of the economic multiplier.   5 marks

	MPC	Multiplier
a	0.5	
b	0.33	
c	0.75	
d	0.6	
e	0.7	

Workbook answers at **www.hoddereducation.co.uk/workbookanswers**

25 For each of the following changes to *AD*, based on the size of the multiplier, calculate the eventual change to national income.   **8 marks**

	Change in *AD*	*MPC*
a	Increase by £65m	0.5
b	Increase by £820m	0.8
c	Increase by £280m	0.75
d	Decrease by £115m	0.6

....

....

....

....

....

....

....

AO3: Analysis

26 Explain two ways in which increases in interest rates affect levels of consumption.   **6 marks**

Worked example

One way in which interest rates affect consumption levels is because of the incentive to save. Interest is paid on any savings placed in a bank account. If this reward for savings is increased (i.e. there are increases in interest rates), then households will be incentivised to save more of their disposable income. Logically, an increase in savings means a lower level of consumption.

> **AO1:** Valid ways identified.

> **AO2:** Basic explanation of how this movement in interest rates (increase) affects consumption.

> **AO3:** Further development of each point into analytical detail.

Another way in which interest rates affect consumption is through the effect on mortgage repayments. Millions of households have purchased their homes by taking out a mortgage. Monthly repayments are made on the mortgage and these include a payment to cover the interest on the mortgage. If interest rates rise, then the monthly mortgage payments will increase (assuming a variable rate mortgage). This means the discretionary income of the household will fall, which means less can be devoted to consumption — i.e. consumption will fall if interest rates rise.

> **AO1:** Valid ways identified.

> **AO2:** Basic explanation of how this movement in interest rates (increase) affects consumption.

> **AO3:** Further development of each point into analytical detail.

27 Explain two factors that would lead to a rise in the level of UK exports. 4 marks

....

....

....

....

28 Explain two factors that would lead to increased UK investment. 6 marks

....

....

....

....

....

....

29 Explain how the size of the multiplier can change over time. 4 marks

....

....

....

....

AO4: Evaluation

Write your answers to these questions on separate sheets of paper and keep them with your workbook.

30 Evaluate the extent to which low interest rates will lead to higher levels of investment. 25 marks

31 To what extent do increases in income lead to higher levels of consumption? 25 marks

Determinants of aggregate supply

After looking at *AD* and the workings of the multiplier, focus is now placed on the level of output produced in an economy, which is measured by aggregate supply (*AS*). *AS* is affected by a number of factors. In the short run, determination of *AS* is based on factors affecting the costs of production for businesses. In the long run, the economy's output is largely determined by the economy's total productive capacity. Alternative models are considered (specifically, the Keynesian *AS* curve).

Practice questions **?**

AO1: Knowledge and understanding

32 Define the term 'short-run aggregate supply' (*SRAS*). 3 marks

....

....

33 Define the term 'long-run aggregate supply' (*LRAS*).   3 marks

....

....

....

34 Explain the main features of the Keynesian *AS* curve.   4 marks

....

....

....

....

35 State whether each of the following changes would shift the *AD* or the *AS* curve:
   a   a fall in indirect taxation
   b   a rise in income tax
   c   lower interest rates
   d   increased productivity
   e   a rise in foreign GDP   5 marks

....

....

....

36 Decide which of the following would shift the *SRAS* curve leftwards and which would shift it rightwards:
   a   a fall in the exchange rate
   b   higher oil prices
   c   falling wage rates
   d   lower indirect taxes
   e   slower growth in productivity   5 marks

....

....

....

37 Explain two factors that would increase *LRAS*.   4 marks

....

....

....

AO2: Application

38 Explain the differences between *SRAS* and *LRAS*.   4 marks

....

....

....

....

39 Draw a diagram to show the effect of a rise in wage rates on the macroeconomic equilibrium.   4 marks

40 Look at the diagram below.

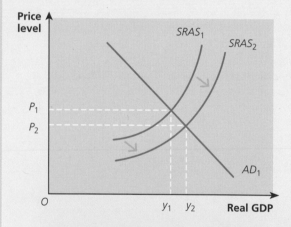

Which of the following could explain the changes shown on the diagram?

a   a rise in productivity

b   a rise in the exchange rate

c   an increase in indirect taxes

d   a decrease in government spending

e   a decrease in exports

f   a decrease in wage rates   3 marks

....

....

....

41 On a diagram, show the effects of an increase in factor mobility on the macroeconomic equilibrium. 4 marks

AO3: Analysis

42 Analyse two effects of a fall in the exchange rate on national income. 6 marks

....
....
....
....
....
....

43 Explain two ways in which a government can increase *LRAS*. 6 marks

....
....
....
....
....

44 Explain, using a diagram, how an increase in *AD* can lead to a government achieving two of its economic objectives. 8 marks

....
....
....
....
....
....
....
....

45 To what extent does spending on infrastructure improve economic performance? **25 marks**

46 To what extent does the *LRAS* curve being vertical mean a government cannot increase economic growth? **25 marks**

Aggregate demand and aggregate supply analysis

The interaction of *AD* and *AS* allows us to determine the equilibrium level of real national income and the price level at that level of output. We can see how changes in the behaviour of the different groups in the economy, such as households, affect the economy's equilibrium position.

AD/AS interaction also affects other macroeconomic variables, such as the unemployment rate, as well as the government's budget and the foreign trade balance.

Practice questions (?)

AO1: Knowledge and understanding

47 Define the term 'demand-side shock'. **3 marks**

....

....

....

48 Explain why the *LRAS* curve is vertical. **3 marks**

....

....

....

49 State whether each of the following would lead to increased or decreased national income.
   a   increased savings
   b   lower direct taxation
   c   higher wage rates
   d   improved transport infrastructure
   e   increased emigration of working population **5 marks**

....

....

....

....

50 State whether each of the following would lead to an increase or decrease in the price level, based on a short-run macroeconomic equilibrium.

  a   increase in government spending

  b   increase in wage rates

  c   increase in productivity

  d   increase in exchange rate   4 marks

....

....

51 Fill in the following table, stating whether there would be an increase or decrease in real GDP and the price level based on the changes to the short-run macroeconomic equilibrium shown in the first column.   4 marks

	Change in real GDP	Change in price level
a Increase in indirect taxation		
b Reduction in government spending		
c Reduction in direct taxation		
d Reduction in wage rates		

52 Each row of the following table makes a statement about the changes that are expected to follow from the change shown in the first column. Decide whether each of the statements is true or false.   4 marks

	Shift in AD/AS	Effect on real GDP	Effect on price level	True or false?
a Increased interest rates	AD decrease	Increase	Decrease	
b Higher indirect taxes	AS decrease	Decrease	Increase	
c Increased productivity	AS increase	Increase	Decrease	
d Lower consumer confidence	AD increase	Decrease	Increase	

AO2: Application

53 Look at the following diagram.

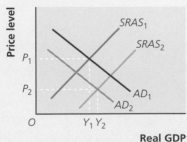

Which of the following changes would explain the change in macroeconomic equilibrium?

  a   an increase in interest rates with lower indirect taxes

  b   an increase in income tax with increased productivity

  c   an increase in exports with lower wage rates

  d   a decrease in government expenditure with an increased exchange rate

  e   a decrease in investment with lower raw material prices

  f   a decrease in savings with increased wage rates   3 marks

....

54 Look at the following diagram.

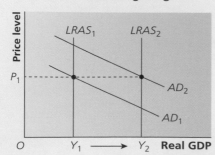

State two pairs of changes in the economy that would cause the change shown in macroeconomic equilibrium.

4 marks

....

....

....

....

....

55 Using a Keynesian *AS* curve, show how increased wage rates can lead to lower real GDP and a higher price level.

4 marks

56 Draw an *AD/AS* diagram to show the effects of a rise in productivity and an increase in government spending on economic activity.

4 marks

AO3: Analysis

57 Explain, using a diagram, how increases in *AD* can be both harmful and good for an economy.

8 marks

Worked example

Increases in *AD* may be harmful if the increase is large relative to the size of the overall *AD*. This is because it could be inflationary. If the economy is operating close to its full employment level (i.e. close to its productive capacity), then increases in *AD* will not result in any significant increases in output. This is because there are few idle resources left to be brought into employment. As a result, businesses are likely to increase prices of goods and services to ration out the excess demand. Repeated across the economy, this is likely to lead to demand-pull inflation. This is shown on the diagram, as the increase in *AD* (from AD_1 to AD_2) leads to a movement up the *AS* curve to a higher price level of P_2 (from P_1, originally).

AO1: A potential harmful effect on the economy is identified — that it might lead to higher inflation.

AO2: There is development applied to the context of the current economic situation.

AO3: The explanation of why higher *AD* leads to inflation is correctly provided and analysed in appropriate detail.

AO3: It is good to link this analysis to a relevant and correctly labelled diagram.

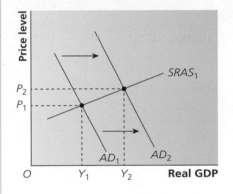

58 Explain, using a diagram, how the reverse multiplier can affect economic performance.   8 marks

59 Explain how the institutional structure of an economy contributes to economic growth.

4 marks

....

....

....

....

60 Using an *AD/AS* diagram, analyse how investment can contribute to economic growth.

9 marks

....

....

....

....

....

....

....

....

....

....

AO4: Evaluation

Write your answers to these questions on separate sheets of paper and keep them with your workbook.

61 To what extent are increases in consumption good for the UK economy?

25 marks

62 Evaluate the extent to which a government can decide what level of GDP it wishes the UK economy to produce.

25 marks

Topic 10: Multiple choice and short answer

1 The diagram below shows a shift from AD_1 to AD_2 in the aggregate demand curve for an economy.

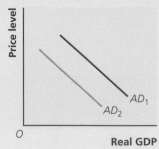

Which of the following would explain the shift in the *AD* curve?

A   lower price level

B   wealth effect of higher house prices

C   fall in the exchange rate

D   lower government expenditure

2   The diagrams below show *AD* and *SRAS* curves for an economy. AD_1 and $SRAS_1$ represent the initial position of the curves. AD_2 and $SRAS_2$ represent shifts in the position of the curves.

A

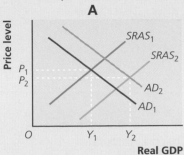

B

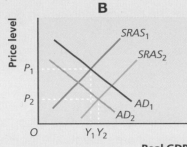

C

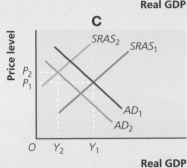

D

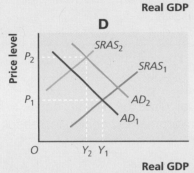

Which one of the diagrams — A, B, C or D — indicates the effect on the economy of a fall in wage rates and a fall in interest rates?

3   The following diagram shows a shift in the *LRAS* of an economy.

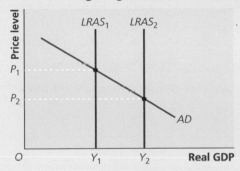

Which of the following would explain the shift in the diagram?

A   improvements in the banking system in the economy

B   increases in welfare benefits

C   reductions in infrastructure projects

D   cuts in wage rates

4   The following diagram shows the *SRAS* and *AD* curves for an economy.

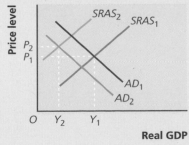

Which of the following would explain the shifts in both curves?

A   a rise in wage rates and an increase in government expenditure

B   a rise in indirect taxation and a rise in investment

C   a rise in the price of raw materials and a rise in income tax

D   an increase in population and a rise in consumer pessimism

5 An economy has a marginal propensity to consume of 0.6. A rise in government expenditure leads to an eventual rise in national income of £375 million.

What was the size of the original increase in government expenditure?

A £150 million

B £75 million

C £225 million

D £62.5 million

6 Government spending increases by £83 billion and, at the same time, exports fall by £8 billion. If national income eventually increases by £325 billion, calculate the size of the multiplier. **2 marks**

....

....

7 The *MPC* is 0.8. Calculate the overall change in real GDP if investment rises by £25 million and government spending increases by £45 million. **2 marks**

....

....

8 Analyse the reasons for a decrease in the level of investment in an economy. **15 marks**

....

....

....

....

....

....

....

....

....

....

....

....

....

....

....

Topic 10: Data response

9 Read Extracts A, B and C and answer the following questions. **40 marks**

Extract A

The UK government is increasingly looking to boost economic growth through increases in its own spending in the UK economy. Successive ministers have promised extra spending on the public sector as a way of boosting economic growth and living standards.

Since the financial crisis, the UK government had undertaken an 'austerity' programme of cuts in government spending, which had imposed harm on many sections of the economy. However, since the 2016 European referendum, there has been a belief that consumer confidence will remain low and the extra government spending will simply replace 'lost' consumer spending.

Even with austerity, consumers have had some help, with interest rates remaining at historically low levels since 2009 — although rate increases are expected in the next few years.

Extract B

Estimates of UK government expenditure

Year	£ billions
2018	842
2016	772
2014	732
2012	683
2010	697
2008	618
2006	552
2004	485

Extract C

Estimating the size of the economic multiplier is not as straightforward as it might seem in economic textbooks. The size of the multiplier is clearly determined by how much spare capacity there is. For example, an economy operating at capacity, or close to capacity, will see a multiplier of almost zero. In a deep recession, the multiplier may grow significantly large in size.

The type of extra spending in the economy may also affect the size of the multiplier. An increase in government expenditure is likely to have a greater effect than a cut in taxes — which may be simply saved by consumers. In the UK, the size of the multiplier is estimated to be somewhere between 0.5 and 1.7.

a Using Extract C, and assuming the highest value estimated for the multiplier, calculate, to two decimal places, the initial change in government spending if it generated an eventual increase in GDP of £25 billion. **2 marks**

....

....

b   Do the data in Extract B support the view that since 2010 the UK government
    has managed to control its own spending?   **4 marks**

....

....

....

....

....

c   Using an appropriate diagram, analyse the impact on the UK economy of
    higher government spending.   **9 marks**

....

....

....

....

....

....

....

....

....

....

d   Evaluate the extent to which increases in interest rates will harm the
    performance of the UK economy.   **25 marks**
    *Write your answer to this question on a separate sheet of paper and keep it
    with your workbook.*

Topic 10: Essay

10 Analyse the determinants of investment in an economy.   **15 marks**   (60)

....

....

....

....

....

....

....

....

....

....

....

....

....

....

....

....

....

....

....

....

....

....

....

....

....

11 To what extent are increases in investment more desirable than increases in
consumption?   **25 marks**

*Write your answer to this question on a separate sheet of paper and keep it with
your workbook.*

Topic 11 Economic performance

Economic growth and the economic cycle

The factors affecting short-run economic growth differ from those affecting long-run growth. It is from short-run growth that an economic cycle emerges. Various explanations have been proposed to account for the economic cycle and this matters as economic performance varies considerably over the different stages of the economic cycle.

Economic shocks also occur, which could have a supply-side or a demand-side cause. These can have unexpected positive or negative consequences for the macroeconomy.

Practice questions ?

AO1: Knowledge and understanding

1 Define the term 'negative output gap'.   3 marks

> **Worked example**
>
> An output gap exists where there is a difference between trend growth and actual growth in the economy and this is negative when actual growth is below the trend rate of economic growth.

AO1: A correct account of an output gap, which is specifically linked to a negative output gap.

2 State the four stages of the economic cycle.   4 marks

....

....

....

....

....

3 Explain what is meant by 'short-run economic growth'.   3 marks

....

....

....

4 Explain what is meant by 'long-run economic growth'.   3 marks

....

....

....

5   Define the term 'trend growth'.   3 marks

....

....

....

6   Identify three economic features of a recession.   3 marks

....

....

....

7   Explain what is meant by sustainable economic growth.   3 marks

....

....

....

AO2: Application

8   Draw a diagram to show trend growth, labelling the axes and clearly showing both
    a positive and negative output gap on the same diagram.   4 marks

9   Draw a diagram of a production possibility curve (*PPC*), showing both short-run
    and long-run growth occurring on the same diagram.   4 marks

10 Divide the following into short-run or long-run causes of economic growth.   5 marks
    a   fall in wage rates
    b   increases in government expenditure
    c   increases in labour supply
    d   advances in technology
    e   fall in direct taxes

....

....

11 State three causes of long-run economic growth.   3 marks

....

....

....

AO3: Analysis

12 Explain two disadvantages of economic growth to individuals.   4 marks

....

....

....

....

13 Using examples, distinguish between short-run and long-run economic growth.   4 marks

....

....

....

....

14 Explain why unemployment is likely to rise during a negative output gap.   4 marks

....

....

....

....

....

15 Explain any two theories put forward to explain fluctuations in the economic cycle.   **8 marks**

....

....

....

....

....

....

....

....

AO4: Evaluation

16 Discuss the extent to which achieving economic growth is desirable in any economy.   **25 marks**

The worked example below shows a model paragraph from a possible response to this question, explaining why growth is desirable. Study this closely and then attempt to answer the question fully on a separate piece of paper.

Worked example

One reason growth is desirable is that it improves the balance on the government's budget. Economic growth, by definition, means that income is rising. This means that revenues from income tax will rise. Given that income is rising, this must necessarily mean that spending is rising — as one person's spending must be another person's income. This means that receipts from taxes on spending, such as VAT, will rise. The rise in tax revenue could be greater than the level of economic growth, given that income taxes in the UK are generally progressive — this means that as people's earnings increase, they move into paying higher rates of tax. At the same time, government spending on welfare, such as on unemployment benefits, may also fall. This is because with economic growth, the derived demand for labour is likely to increase, leading to more people working and fewer unemployed. This means that less needs to be spent by the government. As a result, the budgetary balance on the government's finances will improve. This does assume that the government hasn't used expansionary fiscal policy to achieve the economic growth in the first place, as this may mean that the budget balance worsens rather than improves.

> **AO1:** Relevant reason why economic growth is desirable is identified.

> **AO2:** The reason is applied and then explained as to why growth is desirable.

> **AO3:** Analytical detail is present — looking at how the improvement to the government's finances could vary depending on the structure of taxes.

> **AO4:** Some use of evaluation for this chain of reasoning is included here. Sustained evaluation is a good way of raising your mark.

17 To what extent are fluctuations in economic growth always inevitable?   **25 marks**

Write your answer to this question on a separate sheet of paper and keep it with your workbook.

Employment and unemployment

Minimising unemployment is a key objective of the government. To achieve this, it is important to understand the various causes of unemployment in an economy, relating both to the demand side and supply side of the economy. There are consequences of unemployment for both the individuals and for economic performance, which explains the government's desire to reduce unemployment levels.

AO1: Knowledge and understanding

18 Define the term 'cyclical unemployment'.   3 marks

....

....

....

19 Explain the term 'structural unemployment'.   3 marks

....

....

....

20 Explain the term 'frictional unemployment'.   3 marks

....

....

....

21 State three causes of structural unemployment.   3 marks

....

....

....

22 Explain the term 'voluntary unemployment'.   3 marks

....

....

....

23 Distinguish between demand-side and supply-side causes of unemployment.   4 marks

....

....

....

....

AO2: Application

24 Categorise the following situations as the correct types of unemployment.   4 marks

Situation	Type of unemployment
a Workers looking for work but unwilling to move to the area with job vacancies	
b Workers temporarily unemployed at the same time every year	
c Workers looking for work but lacking the qualifications needed to fill current job vacancies	
d Workers refusing to work at the current wage rate despite job vacancies existing	

25 From the following data, calculate the unemployment rate based on the claimant count and that based on the labour force survey.   4 marks

	In millions
Population of working age	44.0
Economically inactive	9.1
Employed (part-time and full-time)	33.3
Those receiving unemployment benefits	0.6

....

....

....

26 Classify each of the following cases in terms of the correct cause of unemployment:
   a   increased competition from low-cost producers in foreign countries
   b   falling consumer confidence leading to increased savings
   c   higher minimum wage leading to businesses cancelling recruitment
   d   generous benefits offered to those recently becoming unemployed   4 marks

....

....

....

27 Show, on an *AD/AS* diagram, the concept of cyclical unemployment.   4 marks

AO3: Analysis

28 Analyse, using a diagram, why real wage unemployment may increase.　　　　**9 marks**

Worked example

Unemployment can be caused by wages (in real terms) being higher than their free market level. Wages may not fall to the equilibrium level (where labour demand equals labour supply) because they are sticky downwards. This may be caused by features of an economy like powerful trade unions, or through minimum wage legalisation. If the minimum wage is increased significantly, or trade unions find they have more collective bargaining power, then real wage unemployment may increase. This means that the prevailing wage rate may rise even further above the free market equilibrium. This creates an increase in the excess supply of labour as the higher wage rate now means more workers are willing to supply their labour but fewer businesses now demand labour — as the wage rate is now significantly above the marginal revenue product for many businesses. This is shown on the diagram by the actual wage rate rising from W_1 to W_2. As a result, real wage unemployment increases by Q_2Q_3.

> **AO1:** Basic identification of what real wage unemployment is.

> **AO2:** Application of knowledge to how real wages rise above the market-clearing level.

> **AO3:** Analysis of why real wage unemployment may increase, with a good synoptic link here to labour economics from Paper 1 — though this isn't necessary, it is a good approach to use to show full understanding of the overall course.
> Good link to the diagram, illustrating the increase in unemployment.

Diagram: Real wage rate (vertical axis) against Quantity of employment (horizontal axis). Labour supply (upward sloping) and Labour demand (downward sloping). W_2 above W_1. Points Q_2, Q_1, Q_3 on horizontal axis. Real wage unemployment shown between Q_2 and Q_3.

29 Explain two reasons why frictional unemployment may increase.　　　　**4 marks**

....

....

....

....

30 Explain two reasons why structural unemployment may exist in an economy.　　　　**6 marks**

....

....

....

....

31 Outline two consequences of rising unemployment for individuals.   **6 marks**

....

....

....

....

....

....

AO4: Evaluation

32 To what extent can we conclude that unemployment is always the result of there being insufficient demand in the economy?   **25 marks**

The worked example below shows a model conclusion from a possible response to this question. Study this closely and then attempt to answer the question fully on a piece of paper.

Worked example

Some unemployment may be caused by lack of demand in the economy but it is too strong to say that it is always caused by insufficient demand. Unemployment has many causes and it is too simplistic to say that it is always caused by demand-side factors. It might be fair to say that some unemployment is caused by insufficient demand, but not all of it.

Another problem is that it is very difficult for us to conclude what the cause of any unemployment actually is. We can measure the level of unemployment but we cannot be certain what has caused it. Estimates can be made — for example, we may notice that economic growth is above average, which would suggest that it is not the lack of demand that is causing unemployment but some other factor. However, even if growth is above average for the country, this doesn't mean that demand is high enough everywhere. Unemployment varies across the country and therefore lack of demand may explain some of the unemployment in one area, but not in another.

It is likely that at any time there are multiple causes of unemployment in existence within the economy. In the time of a recession, much of the unemployment is due to insufficient demand, but it is still likely to be the case that frictional, structural and real wage factors are also present in creating unemployment. Therefore we cannot conclude that unemployment is always due to the lack of demand in the economy.

AO4: A good start to the overall conclusion is to look at the strength of the statement being evaluated. In this case, it is asking if insufficient demand is always the explanation for unemployment. Using the word 'always' is difficult to justify as it would mean, in this case, that it is the only real explanation for unemployment — which we know not to be the case.

AO4: This is an excellent point — that it is difficult to pinpoint the exact cause of unemployment. Causes can be estimated but these will never be entirely accurate. This evaluative point is developed to suggest how we might discover whether lack of demand is the cause.

AO4: Recognition here that there are multiple causes and that the predominant cause of unemployment will vary over the economic cycle.

AO4: Always good to link back to the original title and make a final judgement.

33 'The costs of unemployment to the individual are so high that reduction of unemployment should be the prime objective of any government.' Do you agree with this statement? Justify your view.

    25 marks

    Write your answer to this question on a separate sheet of paper and keep it with your workbook.

34 To what extent can unemployment be eliminated in the long run through structural reform to the economy?

    25 marks

    Write your answer to this question on a separate sheet of paper and keep it with your workbook.

Inflation and deflation

Keeping inflation on target (1–3%) is another key economic objective. Although low inflation is seen as desirable, governments also wish to avoid deflation, as both have potentially harmful consequences for individuals and the economy as a whole (though there are some cases where inflation and deflation may not be problematic).

To manage the levels of both inflation and deflation, it is important to know their causes — and there are multiple causes, including one related to the money supply.

Practice questions ?

AO1: Knowledge and understanding

35 State two causes of inflation.

    2 marks

    ....

    ....

36 Define the term 'deflation'.

    3 marks

    ....

    ....

37 Define the term 'disinflation'.

    3 marks

    ....

    ....

    ....

38 Define the term 'cost-push inflation'.

    3 marks

    ....

    ....

    ....

39 What is meant by the term 'velocity of circulation'? 3 marks

....

....

....

40 Explain the relevance of the quantity theory of money. 4 marks

....

....

....

....

AO2: Application

41 From the following data, identify any years in which the economy experienced deflation or disinflation. 3 marks

Year	Price index for year
1	109
2	107
3	111
4	114
5	117

Worked example

Inflation is calculated as the percentage change in the price level over a period of 1 year.

Inflation in each year:

Year 2 = (107 − 109)/109 × 100 = −1.8%

Year 3 = (111 − 107)/107 × 100 = 3.7%

Year 4 = (114 − 111)/111 × 100 = 2.7%

Year 5 = (117 − 114)/114 × 100 = 2.6%

Deflation: in year 2

Disinflation: in year 4 and year 5

> **AO2:** The inflation rate is calculated for each year (years 2–5) and this allows a decision to be made on whether it is deflation or disinflation.

42 With a base year index of 100 in year 1, the index numbers for year 2 are as follows: money supply: 107; price level: 104; real national output: 108.

Using the quantity theory of money, calculate the index number for the velocity of circulation in year 2 to the nearest whole number. 2 marks

....

....

43 Show the effect of demand-pull inflation on an *AD/AS* diagram.   4 marks

44 Show the effect of benign deflation on an *AD/AS* diagram.   4 marks

AO3: Analysis

45 Explain the effect of expectations on changes in the price level.   4 marks

....

....

....

....

46 Explain two reasons why inflation is harmful for an economy.   6 marks

....

....

....

....

....

47 Explain how commodity prices affect inflation.   6 marks

....

....

....

....

....

48 Explain how the quantity theory of money can explain inflation in an economy.   4 marks

....

....

....

....

....

....

AO4: Evaluation

Write your answers to these questions on separate sheets of paper and keep them with your workbook.

49 Evaluate whether deflation is always harmful for an economy.   25 marks

50 Evaluate whether reducing inflation to low levels is always worthwhile.   25 marks

Policy conflicts

There often appears to be a trade-off in terms of achieving either low inflation or low unemployment, but not both at the same time. This trade-off can be represented in the short-run Phillips curve. It is suggested that the trade-off between inflation and unemployment does not exist in the long run. There are other policy conflicts that can exist in the economy.

Practice questions ?

AO1: Knowledge and understanding

51 Explain the term 'policy conflict'.   3 marks

....

....

....

52 Distinguish between the short-run and long-run Phillips curves.   4 marks

....

....

....

....

53 Explain the term 'money illusion'.   3 marks

....

....

....

54 Explain the term 'adaptive expectations'.   3 marks

....

....

....

AO2: Application

55 Describe two distinct policy conflicts.   4 marks

....

....

....

....

56 Draw a diagram to show an economy moving from the short-run to the long-run Phillips curve.   4 marks

AO3: Analysis

57 Using a diagram, explain how the trade-off shown on the short-run Phillips curve may not exist in the long run.   9 marks

....

....

....

....

....

....

....

....

58 'In the long run, the economy will always return to its natural rate of unemployment, which means there is no point in attempting to reduce unemployment.'

Explain the reasoning behind the above statement and why it may be based on mistaken understanding.

9 marks

....

....

....

....

....

....

....

....

....

....

....

....

....

....

....

....

....

AO4: Evaluation

Write your answers to these questions on separate sheets of paper and keep them with your workbook.

59 To what extent is there a trade-off between achieving low unemployment and low inflation?

25 marks

60 Evaluate the usefulness of achieving high economic growth for a government.

25 marks

Topic 11: Multiple choice and short answer

65

1 The short-run Phillips curve illustrates the relationship between:

   A the price level and the level of unemployment

   B the rate of economic growth and the rate of inflation

   C the rate of inflation and the rate of unemployment

   D the wage rate growth and the rate of employment

2 The following diagram shows actual and trend economic growth.

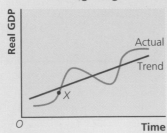

   At point *X*, which of the following combinations of unemployment and inflation is most likely to occur?

	Inflation	Unemployment
A	Above average	Above average
B	Above average	Below average
C	Below average	Above average
D	Below average	Below average

3 A problem that exists as a result of rising demand-pull inflation would include which of the following?

   A uncompetitive exports

   B consumers deferring purchases

   C rising real cost of debt

   D falling output

4 Rising prices, falling unemployment and a growing trade deficit are normally found in which stage of the economic cycle?

   A recovery

   B boom

   C recession

   D downturn

5 Based on the quantity theory of money, which of the following is most likely to lead to higher prices?

   A rising velocity of circulation, while output and money supply remain constant

   B rising money supply, while velocity of circulation falls and output remains constant

   C rising output and money supply, while velocity of circulation falls

   D rising money supply, while output increases and velocity of circulation falls significantly

6 The index of consumer prices rises over a period of 1 year from 189.4 to 192.3.
   To one decimal place, calculate the inflation rate at the end of this period.   **2 marks**

....

....

7   From the following information, calculate the unemployment rate to one
     decimal place.   2 marks

	In millions
Working population	35.6
Employed (part time and full time)	34.1

....

....

8   Analyse possible causes of long-run economic growth in the UK.   9 marks

....

....

....

....

....

....

....

....

....

....

....

9   Analyse voluntary and involuntary causes of unemployment.   9 marks

....

....

....

....

....

....

....

....

....

10 Analyse the causes of deflation in an economy.   **15 marks**

....

....

....

....

....

....

....

....

....

....

....

....

....

....

....

....

Exam-style questions ?

Topic 11: Data response

11 Read Extracts A, B and C and answer the following questions.   **40 marks**

Extract A

The data here relate to both inflation and unemployment calculations in the UK.
Table 1 contains data relating to the consumer price index (CPI) used to calculate
UK inflation. Table 2 compares the inflation rate and the unemployment rate in the UK
from 2009 to 2018.

Table 1 UK CPI, September 2018–September 2019

2018 SEP	106.6	2019 APR	107.6
2018 OCT	106.7	2019 MAY	107.9
2018 NOV	107.0	2019 JUN	107.9
2018 DEC	107.1	2019 JUL	107.9
2019 JAN	106.3	2019 AUG	108.4
2019 FEB	106.8	2019 SEP	108.5
2019 MAR	107.0		

Source: ONS

Table 2 UK inflation rate and unemployment rate, 2009–18

Year	Inflation rate (%)	Unemployment rate (%)
2009	2.2	7.6
2010	3.3	7.9
2011	4.5	8.1
2012	2.8	8.0
2013	2.6	7.6
2014	1.5	6.2
2015	0.0	5.4
2016	0.7	4.9
2017	2.7	4.4
2018	2.5	4.1

Source: ONS

Extract B

For many years, UK inflation was seen as the biggest challenge facing the government. During the last 40 years, it has been argued that the recessions faced by the UK were worsened and, in some cases, caused by the government of the day attempting to get inflation under control.

High inflation during the 1970s and 1980s certainly led to interest rates being higher than they otherwise would have been, thus creating higher repayments each month for those making mortgage repayments. There are other costs also associated with high inflation.

In 2015, the UK economy experienced something that had not been seen for almost 80 years — a period of time of falling prices as measured by the official price index, the CPI. Although inflation is considered to be bad for an economy in many ways, a period of deflation could also lead to a number of economic problems emerging.

It is the Bank of England's job to keep inflation close to the central target of 2%. Normally, the way to increase the rate of inflation would be to reduce the Bank of England's base rate, but this rate has already been close to zero (lower than 1% since 2009) and cannot be realistically reduced any lower.

Extract C

If inflation is kept on target and the problems of high inflation and deflation are avoided, the government can turn its attention to other economic objectives. Before inflation became a major problem, the UK government saw full employment as its prime objective. Unemployment generates many problems for both individuals and for the government and it is only right that a government should attempt to reduce unemployment levels.

Some say there is a trade-off between inflation and unemployment in that the objectives for these variables cannot both be achieved at the same time. Others disagree and say that both low inflation and low unemployment can be achieved together as long as the proper policies are used in the correct manner.

a Using the data in Extract A, calculate, to one decimal place, the inflation rate in the year to September 2019 based on the CPI. **2 marks**

....

....

....

b Do the data in Table 2 of Extract A support the relationship between unemployment and inflation suggested by the short-run Phillip's curve? **4 marks**

....

....

....

....

c Analyse the economic reasons why a government would want to achieve low unemployment. **9 marks**

....

....

....

....

....

....

....

....

....

....

d Economists argue that deflation needs to be avoided as much as inflation. Evaluate the view that deflation is potentially even more harmful than inflation for an economy. **25 marks**

Write your answer to this question on a separate sheet of paper and keep it with your workbook.

Topic 11: Essay

12 Analyse the potential policy conflicts that exist in an economy.   **15 marks**   60

....

....

....

....

....

....

....

....

....

....

....

....

....

....

....

....

....

....

....

....

....

....

....

....

....

13 To what extent should a government aim for full employment?   **25 marks**

Write your answer to this question on a separate sheet of paper and keep it with your workbook.

Topic 12 Financial markets and monetary policy

The structure of financial markets and financial assets

Money serves a number of functions and must have a number of characteristics for it to function effectively. Different financial markets exist to channel money from those with more than they currently need to those looking to acquire more money than they currently have. Methods of acquiring finance for most businesses involve a combination of debt and equity.

Practice questions ?

AO1: Knowledge and understanding

1 State the four functions of money.   4 marks

....

....

....

....

2 State five characteristics something must have for it to be accepted as 'money'.   5 marks

....

....

....

....

....

3 Explain the term 'money supply'.   3 marks

....

....

....

4 Distinguish between narrow and broad money.   4 marks

....

....

....

....

5 Explain what is meant by the term 'the money market'. 3 marks

....

....

....

6 Explain what is meant by the term 'the foreign exchange market'. 3 marks

....

....

....

AO2: Application

7 Arrange the following items into a spectrum of liquidity, starting with the least liquid first. 5 marks

Cash — Property — Treasury bills — Bank balance — Shares

....

....

8 A bond has a current market price of £160 and its annual coupon is £4.50. Calculate the yield on this bond to one decimal place. 2 marks

....

....

9 A government bond has a face value of £100. The annual coupon is £4. The maturity date for the bond is many years away. The current yield on the bond is 2.5%. Calculate the market price of the bond. 2 marks

....

....

10 Match each of the following functions to the correct financial market: money market, capital market or foreign exchange market.

a   Helps companies to float on the stock market.

b   Makes arrangements for companies that want to buy foreign currency at some point in the future.

c   Facilitates trade in debentures between companies.

d   Provides short-term finance to individuals. 4 marks

....

....

....

....

AO3: Analysis

11 Explain the differences between debt and equity. **6 marks**

Worked example

One difference is that a business which borrows money and takes on debt has to pay interest on that debt. This means that even if the business is not performing well and not generating much profit, it still has to make payments to the lender. Equity carries no interest charges — the business may pay dividends to the shareholders but only if it feels it can afford to do so. It is under no obligation to pay dividends.

> AO1: Relevant points identified.

> AO2: Applied to the context of financial markets (e.g. banks).

> AO3: Relevant development and explanation now provided for each point.

Another difference is that those purchasing equity in a business have some input into the running of the business. Holders of equity are known as shareholders and they are able to vote at the company's annual general meetings and can be involved in the decision making within the business — the shareholders are the true owners of a company. Those lending money to the business have no such power.

> AO1: Relevant points identified.

> AO2: Applied to the context of financial markets (e.g. banks).

> AO3: Relevant development and explanation now provided for each point.

12 Explain two functions of the capital market. **6 marks**

....

....

....

....

13 Distinguish between the spot and forward markets in the foreign exchange market. **4 marks**

....

....

....

14 Analyse the roles of the money market, the capital market and the foreign exchange market. **9 marks**

....

....

....

....

....

....

....

Commercial banks and investment banks

There are various types of bank that exist in the economy. These include commercial banks, which create credit from relending customers' deposits. Investment banks exist to serve other businesses and other banks. The structure of these banks is different from that of most other businesses. These banks have various different objectives, which can create potential conflicts.

Practice questions ❓

AO1: Knowledge and understanding

15 State three functions of a commercial bank.   **3 marks**

....

....

....

16 Explain the difference between a commercial bank and an investment bank.   **4 marks**

....

....

....

....

....

....

17 Define the term 'equity' in the context of finance for banks and businesses. **3 marks**

....

....

18 Explain the term 'debenture'.   **3 marks**

....

....

....

19 Explain what is meant by the term 'fractional banking'.   **3 marks**

....

....

....

20 Explain what information is shown on a bank's balance sheet. 3 marks

....

....

....

AO2: Application

21 The following are found on the balance sheet of a commercial bank. Rearrange them so that they are in the correct order of decreasing liquidity. 5 marks

Most liquid				Least liquid
Money at call	Advances	Bonds	Cash	Property

....

....

22 Categorise the following into either assets or liabilities of a commercial bank. 5 marks

Notes and coins	Deposits	Share capital	Bills	Balances at central bank

....

....

23 Divide the following into the objectives and the functions of a commercial bank:

  a   ensuring sufficient liquidity

  b   providing efficient payment systems

  c   accepting deposits from customers

  d   attaining profitability

  e   lending to economic agents 5 marks

....

....

24 Divide the following into activities of a commercial bank and activities of an investment bank:

  a   currency speculation on foreign exchange markets

  b   assessing the riskiness of those wishing to borrow money

  c   assisting businesses by providing banking services

  d   assisting businesses by organising share issues

  e   trading in securities 5 marks

....

....

Workbook answers at **www.hoddereducation.co.uk/workbookanswers**

AO3: Analysis

25 Explain two functions of a commercial bank.   4 marks

....

....

....

....

26 Explain two objectives of a commercial bank.   4 marks

....

....

....

....

27 Explain one conflict between the different objectives of a commercial bank.   4 marks

....

....

....

....

....

28 Explain how a commercial bank can create credit.   4 marks

....

....

....

....

AO4: Evaluation

29 Evaluate the extent to which the government can actually control the
money supply.   25 marks

*Write your answer to this question on a separate sheet of paper and keep it with
your workbook.*

Central banks and monetary policy

Central banks exist to maintain financial and economic stability. Financial stability is maintained through monitoring and regulating the financial markets of the economy. Economic stability exists through careful implementation of monetary policy. Monetary policy is primarily concerned with interest rate management, which is performed by the Monetary Policy Committee (MPC) of the Bank of England. Monetary policy also includes other instruments used to keep economic performance on a stable trajectory.

AO1: Knowledge and understanding

30 Define the term 'monetary policy'. *3 marks*

Worked example

Monetary policy refers to manipulation of the price and availability of money within an economy to achieve economic objectives — usually enacted through changes in interest rates.

> **AO1:** This answer covers the necessary aspects of monetary policy. It refers to interest rates (the 'price' of obtaining money) and the money supply, and to the fact that monetary policy is a policy used to achieve the goals of the government. It then notes that interest rates are one aspect of monetary policy. It could also have included exchange rates, credit availability and quantitative easing as other examples.

31 Define the term 'quantitative easing'. *3 marks*

....

....

....

32 Explain what is meant by the bank rate. *3 marks*

....

....

....

33 Explain the term 'lender of last resort'. *4 marks*

....

....

....

....

34 Explain the role of the Monetary Policy Committee (MPC). *3 marks*

....

....

....

35 Explain what is meant by the term 'transmission mechanism'. 3 marks

....

....

....

AO2: Application

36 State whether the MPC would consider increasing or decreasing the bank rate in each of the following situations:

   a   high consumer confidence leading to increased borrowing

   b   increased business failure occurring across the economy

   c   falling unemployment

   d   falling price level   4 marks

....

....

37 Which of the following would be likely to occur in the first 2 years after a significant rise in the bank rate?

   a   reduction in inflation

   b   increased borrowing by consumers

   c   reduced unemployment

   d   increased trade surplus

   e   increased business investment   5 marks

....

....

38 Explain how increases in the bank rate create two potential policy conflicts. 4 marks

....

....

....

....

....

39 On an *AD/AS* diagram, show the effects of lower interest rates on macroeconomic performance. 4 marks

AO3: Analysis

40 Explain two functions of a central bank. *4 marks*

....

....

....

....

41 Analyse how quantitative easing can bring about an economic recovery. *6 marks*

....

....

....

....

....

....

....

42 Explain three ways in which the transmission mechanism of monetary policy works in the economy. *9 marks*

....

....

....

....

....

....

....

....

....

....

....

Workbook answers at **www.hoddereducation.co.uk/workbookanswers**

43 Explain two limitations of using interest rates to control macroeconomic performance. **6 marks**

....

....

....

....

....

AO4: Evaluation

44 To what extent does monetary policy fail to work when interest rates reach near-zero levels? **25 marks**

The worked example below shows a model paragraph from a possible response to this question, explaining why monetary policy is less effective at low interest rate levels. Study this closely and then attempt to answer the question fully on a separate piece of paper.

Worked example

One way in which monetary policy fails to work is that interest rates cannot be reduced below zero. This is because a negative interest rate would mean that people were paid to borrow money and were charged by banks for savings. This would create undesirable incentives in that people would want to borrow more money than is sensible and debt levels would increase. At the same time, people would be reluctant to save and be less likely to use banks to save their money if they were charged for it. This could create problems. Banks need customers' savings in order to lend to other businesses. In addition, if economic growth is low and unemployment is increasing, then stimulus is needed in the economy and interest rates cannot practically be lowered any further. As a result, monetary policy does fail when interest rates reach near-zero levels. However, some countries have experimented with negative interest rates in order to stimulate their economies.

AO1: Problem of near-zero interest rates identified — i.e. they cannot easily be lowered any further.

AO2: Application of problem of negative interest rates is explained.

AO3: Analysis of the economic issues of negative interest rates.

AO3: A link back to the question is given here, with mention of the effect on economic objectives.

AO4: A brief evaluative point is made here — useful for a top-mark answer.

45 Evaluate the extent to which a government can achieve its objectives using monetary policy alone. **25 marks**

Write your answer to this question on a separate sheet of paper and keep it with your workbook.

Regulation of the financial system

Since the 2007–8 financial crisis, the UK government and the Bank of England have sought to keep tighter control over the financial sector of the economy. This has involved the creation of new regulatory authorities and new methods of ensuring that private sector banks do not take unnecessary risks. It is a careful balancing act, as the UK's financial sector makes a significant contribution to UK GDP but also places the deposits of millions of customers at risk if it fails.

Practice questions ?

AO1: Knowledge and understanding

46 State the three institutions set up to improve financial stability after the financial crash of 2007–8.

3 marks

....

....

....

47 Explain what is meant by the term 'stress test'.

3 marks

....

....

....

48 Distinguish between macroprudential and microprudential regulation.

4 marks

....

....

....

....

49 What is meant by the term 'systematic risk'?

3 marks

....

....

....

50 In the context of banking, what is a liquidity ratio?

3 marks

....

....

....

AO2: Application

51 In the context of the banking system, explain the term 'moral hazard'. **4 marks**

Worked example

Moral hazard refers to the situation where someone (or an organisation) takes too many risks, knowing that they will not have to face the full negative consequences if a risk fails. In the context of the banking system, this would occur if banks engaged in risky lending and speculation knowing that the government would 'bail them out' should they fail as businesses.

A01: Correct explanation of moral hazard.

A02: Good link to the banking system. This contributed to the financial crisis — many accused commercial and investment banks of taking too many risks with their customers' money, knowing that the government would never allow banks to fail.

52 Link each regulatory authority to the correct statement about that authority. **3 marks**

Regulatory authority	Statement
a Prudential Regulation Authority	1 It should take action to remove systematic risks to the financial system.
b Financial Policy Committee	2 It protects consumers by ensuring healthy competition between financial institutions.
c Financial Conduct Authority	3 It monitors individual financial institutions and can impose capital and liquidity ratios on them.

AO3: Analysis

53 Analyse the potential causes of a financial crisis. **9 marks**

....

....

....

....

....

....

....

....

....

....

....

....

....

54 Explain three ways in which financial regulation has been implemented in the UK since 2010.

9 marks

....

....

....

....

....

....

....

....

....

....

....

55 Explain how capital and liquidity ratios could help regulate a financial system.

6 marks

....

....

....

....

....

....

....

....

AO4: Evaluation

Write your answers to these questions on separate sheets of paper and keep them with your workbook.

56 To what extent can interest rates be used to achieve economic stability?

25 marks

57 To what extent does financial regulation make it impossible for a financial crisis to happen again?

25 marks

Topic 12: Multiple choice and short answer

50

1 A bond is issued with a nominal value of £100 and the annual coupon is £2. When the bond was issued, it offered a return that was similar to other comparable securities. Three years later, the market rate of interest has fallen to 0.5%. This bond will not mature for many years yet. Calculate the approximate market price of this bond.

   A £50

   B £400

   C £200

   D £80

2 Which of the following would not be classed as a liability of a commercial bank?

   A share capital issued

   B deposits by customers

   C long-term borrowing

   D loans made to customers

3 Which of the following types of bank is responsible for controlling the money supply in an economy?

   A commercial bank

   B investment bank

   C central bank

   D wholesale bank

4 Which of the following does the Bank of England's 'lender of last resort' function cover?

   A provision of liquidity to failing non-financial businesses during a recession

   B provision of liquidity to a bank that has mismanaged its finances

   C provision of liquidity to the private sector during a financial crisis

   D provision of liquidity to the banking system to meet the shortfalls in the banking system

5 Which of the following would not be included in the assets of a commercial bank?

   A cash

   B balances at the Bank of England

   C government debt held

   D reserves (e.g. retained profits)

6 A bond that had an original price of £100 now has a current market price of £80 and also has a yield of 5%. Calculate its annual coupon.   **2 marks**

   ....

   ....

   ....

7 The initial price of a bond was £100 and its coupon was £2.50. The redemption date on this bond is many years away. Calculate the likely market price of this bond if the current yield on other bonds is 1.5%.   **2 marks**

   ....

   ....

   ....

8 Analyse the impact of lower interest rates on the UK economy.   **15 marks**

....

....

....

....

....

....

....

....

....

....

....

....

....

....

....

....

....

....

....

....

....

....

....

....

....

Topic 12: Data response

9 Read Extracts A, B and C and answer the following questions.   **40 marks**

Extract A

Year	% change
2010	1.9
2011	1.5
2012	1.5
2013	2.1
2014	2.6
2015	2.4
2016	1.9
2017	1.9
2018	1.4
2019	1.2

Economic growth, 2010–19 (annual % change in GDP)

Decade	Growth (%)
1980s	2.7
1990s	2.2
2000s	1.8

Average UK economic growth per decade

Extract B

Interest rates are often seen as the main component of UK economy policy. Since 1997, UK interest rates have been set by the Bank of England independently of government decision making. The 'operational' independence of the UK's central bank has meant greater success in achieving low inflation. In addition, the inflation target of 2% is set so that it encourages interest rates to be cut if it is felt inflation might get too low — thus helping to boost economic growth when inflation is not a threat.

Since the financial crisis, UK interest rates have been kept at historically low levels (under 1% since 2009). This is believed to boost economic activity — although some believe growth would have been higher if the government had not launched a drastic round of cuts in government spending.

Others also suggest that tighter regulation of the financial system has placed unnecessarily tight restrictions on banks, which may harm economic activity.

Extract C

Apart from low interest rates, the government has used a number of schemes to stimulate the economy after the financial crisis. The Funding for Lending Scheme (FLS) was a way of allowing banks to access money at very low interest rates, which would encourage banks to lend money to businesses at similarly low interest rates.

Quantitative easing (QE) may also have helped. This is a system whereby the Bank of England injects more money into the economy by buying assets from commercial banks and other institutions. This means that they have more liquid resources and are more willing to lend out. QE was seen as particularly important given that commercial banks were reluctant to lend out money even though interest rates have been very low.

a Calculate the average (mean) rate of economic growth for the period 2010–19 to one decimal place.

2 marks

....

....

b Do the data in Extract A support the view that low interest rates have boosted economic activity?

4 marks

....

....

....

....

c Using a diagram, analyse how tighter financial regulation may affect UK economic performance.

9 marks

....

....

....

....

....

....

....

d To what extent have low interest rates alone sustained the UK's economic recovery?

25 marks

Write your answer to this question on a separate sheet of paper and keep it with your workbook.

Topic 12: Essay

10 Analyse the methods used by a government to achieve financial stability.   **15 marks**

60

....

....

....

....

....

....

....

....

....

....

....

....

....

....

....

....

....

....

....

....

....

....

....

....

....

11 To what extent should the government support the commercial banking sector of the UK?   **25 marks**

Write your answer to this question on a separate sheet of paper and keep it with your workbook.

Topic 13 Fiscal policy and supply-side policies

Fiscal policy

Government spending occurs for a number of reasons and is financed through a variety of taxes — also levied for a number of reasons (and not just to fund government spending). Governments regularly spend more than they collect in tax and this has a number of implications for the economy. The budget balance and its relationship with national debt matters as it can affect the rest of the economy.

AO1: Knowledge and understanding

1 Give two examples of direct taxes and indirect taxes used in the UK.

4 marks

Direct taxes	Indirect taxes

2 Define the term 'fiscal policy'.

3 marks

....

....

3 Define the term 'progressive tax'.

3 marks

....

....

4 Explain one function of the Office for Budget Responsibility (OBR).

2 marks

....

....

5 Define the term 'regressive tax'.

3 marks

....

....

6 Define the term 'contractionary fiscal policy'.

3 marks

....

....

7 Define the term 'structural budget deficit'.

3 marks

....

....

8 Define the term 'cyclical budget surplus'. 3 marks

....

....

AO2: Application

9 If someone earns $65,000 and is taxed at 10% on the first $30,000 and at 20% on any further income, calculate how much tax they would pay. 4 marks

Worked example

20% tax paid on ($65,000 – $30,000) = $7,000

10% tax paid on $30,000 = $3,000

Total tax paid = $10,000

> **AO2:** The student recognises that the 20% rate is only paid on income in excess of $30,000 and any income below this is taxed at 10%.

10 A person earns £15,000. Tax is payable on incomes in excess of £12,500 at a rate of 20%. How much tax do they pay? 2 marks

....

....

11 A person earns $50,000 in 1 year. Income tax is levied at 25% but there is a tax-free personal allowance of $10,000. Calculate how much income tax this person would pay. 2 marks

....

....

12 The following table summarises the direct tax bands for income earned in the UK in 2020–21.

Tax rate	Income range
Personal allowance (tax free)	£0–£12,500
Basic rate (20%)	£12,500–£50,000
Higher rate (40%)	£50,000–£150,000
Additional rate (45%)	£150,000+

Calculate the amounts of income tax paid by those earning the following amounts:

a £18,000 2 marks

....

....

....

b £37,500 2 marks

....

....

....

c £70,000 3 marks

....

....

....

d £200,000 4 marks

....

....

....

AO3: Analysis

13 Using a diagram, explain how an increase in indirect taxes can lead to a lower
level of economic activity. 6 marks

Worked example

Increased indirect taxes affect the profitability of production. If
there is a higher indirect tax on a product, then this means the
profitability of output is reduced as some of the selling price is
passed to the government instead of being kept by the business.
If this is repeated on all output, then the increase in indirect
taxes leads to a lower level of production in the economy due
to the reduced profitability. This means that at all price levels,
businesses will reduce output and the *SRAS* curve will shift to
the left (shown on the diagram as $SRAS_1$ to $SRAS_2$). This leads to
an increased price level and also a lower level of real GDP (now
at P_2, Y_2), i.e. there is a lower level of economic activity.

AO1: Effect of increased taxes identified.

AO2: Explanation of how indirect taxes affect businesses developed.

AO3: Good link to a correctly drawn and labelled diagram.

14 Explain one way in which increases in government spending will reduce unemployment. 4 marks

....

....

....

15 Explain two ways fiscal policy can be used to reduce income inequality.   6 marks

....

....

....

....

....

....

16 Analyse two effects of an increase in direct taxation on economic performance.   8 marks

....

....

....

....

....

....

....

....

17 Analyse, with the use of a diagram, why a government may increase taxation in the UK.   9 marks

....

....

....

....

....

18 Assess whether a government should always aim for a balanced budget. 25 marks

Write your answer to this question on a separate sheet of paper and keep it with your workbook.

19 Assess whether decreases in direct taxation will lead to improved economic performance. 25 marks

Write your answer to this question on a separate sheet of paper and keep it with your workbook.

Supply-side policy

Long-run growth comes from increases in the economy's productive capacity and is shown by rightward shifts in the *LRAS* curve. This is referred to as the supply side of the economy. Increases in the productive capacity of an economy can come from general supply-side improvements or specific supply-side policies. Supply-side policies are implemented by the government to increase long-run growth in the economy and this will also affect the level of unemployment, the level of inflation and the foreign trade balance. Supply-side improvements come from 'natural' increases in the productive capacity through profit-seeking behaviour within the private sector.

Practice questions ?

AO1: Knowledge and understanding

20 Define the term 'supply-side improvement'. 3 marks

> **Worked example**
>
> A supply-side improvement occurs when there is an expansion of the economy's productive capacity that does not come from deliberate government policy and results from 'natural' changes in the economy — for example, more entrepreneurial activity occurring naturally.

AO1: Clear definition that covers the supply-side aspect and also the fact that it is not the result of a policy change that increases the *LRAS*.

21 Define the term 'supply-side policy'. 3 marks

....

....

22 State one example each of a supply-side policy and a supply-side improvement. 2 marks

....

....

23 Explain what is meant by a 'flexible labour market'. 3 marks

....

....

....

24 Explain what is meant by 'free market supply-side policies'.   3 marks

....

....

....

25 Explain what is meant by 'interventionist supply-side policies'.   3 marks

....

....

....

26 In the context of supply-side policies, explain what is meant by the term 'deregulation'.   3 marks

....

....

....

AO2: Application

27 Explain how income tax reductions can increase both *AD* and *AS* at the same time.   4 marks

....

....

....

28 Explain the Laffer curve's relevance to supply-side policies.   4 marks

....

....

....

29 Explain the term 'supply-side fiscal policy', giving two examples.   3 marks

....

....

....

30 Classify each of the following as either a free market or an interventionist supply-side policy.

  a   deregulation of industries

  b   subsidies for research and development

  c   reductions in trade union power

  d   educational reform   4 marks

....

....

....

....

31 Explain how investment in a new high-speed railway would lead to an increase in the *LRAS* curve.   4 marks

....

....

....

....

AO3: Analysis

32 Explain, using a diagram, how lower direct tax rates can lead to supply-side benefits for an economy.   6 marks

Worked example

One benefit is that lower direct taxes increase the incentive to work. If people are taxed less on their incomes (i.e. lower direct tax rates), then this makes working more attractive as each hour worked is more 'profitable' for the individual. As a result, people either choose to work rather than be voluntarily unemployed or choose to increase the hours worked. The increase in labour supply means that the *LRAS* curve shifts to the right (shown by $LRAS_1$ to $LRAS_2$) and this leads to a higher level of real GDP at a lower price level.

AO1: Valid reason identified — the 'incentive' argument.

AO2: Logical chain of reasoning is developed.

AO3: Clear link with economic performance via a correct and fully labelled diagram.

33 Explain two ways in which interventionist supply-side policies can increase long-run growth.

6 marks

....

....

....

....

....

....

34 Explain two limitations of using suppy-side policies to improve macroeconomic performance.

6 marks

....

....

....

....

....

....

35 Analyse, using a diagram, how free-market supply-side policies lead to lower unemployment.

9 marks

....

....

....

....

....

....

36 Analyse, using a diagram, how changes in government expenditure can improve supply-side performance in an economy.　　　　**9 marks**

....

....

....

....

....

AO4: Evaluation

37 To what extent can supply-side policies alone lead to lower unemployment?　　**25 marks**

The worked example below shows a model conclusion from a possible response to this question. Study this closely and then attempt to answer the question fully on a separate piece of paper.

Worked example

Overall, supply-side policies alone cannot lead to lower unemployment. This is because not all causes of unemployment are due to problems with the supply side of the economy. As discussed in this essay, structural and frictional unemployment can be dealt with through supply-side policies, and other types of unemployment can also be reduced through this method. However, if we are in recession, the lack of demand is more than likely to contribute to the level of unemployment that probably exists — and this requires a boost to *AD* to solve it.

There is also the issue that it can take a long time for supply-side policies to lower unemployment, so they may work, but may take years to have their full effect on unemployment. This happened in the UK when the government implemented many supply-side policies in the 1980s, but unemployment only fell to very low levels from the late 1990s onwards.

> **AO4:** Good start — challenging the question's assertion.

> **AO4:** Justification of earlier assertion, by noting that some unemployment is caused by lack of demand (rather than by problems with the supply side).

> **AO4:** This is an evaluative point — perhaps not exactly answering the question but showing how supply-side policies do not always work as quickly as other policies.

Having said that, there are some supply-side policies that also boost *AD* at the same time. These would include investment in infrastructure — which can help lower structural unemployment but also lead to higher *AD*. In this case, supply-side policies might also reduce cyclical unemployment at the same time. So overall, we need to be more specific about what kind of supply-side policies we are referring to. Therefore the correct answer is that it depends on the type of supply-side policy we are considering — some, alone, can reduce unemployment of all kinds, whereas others cannot.

A04: Excellent point here — starting to show that the essay title has more levels of complexity than might be initially thought.

38 Evaluate the usefulness of supply-side policies in boosting economic growth.　　**25 marks**

Write your answer to this question on a separate sheet of paper and keep it with your workbook.

Exam-style questions

Topic 13: Multiple choice and short answer

1 In which situation would contractionary fiscal policy be the most appropriate policy?

　　A increased budget surplus

　　B negative output gap growing

　　C increased trade surplus

　　D inflationary pressure emerging

2 Which of the following is an example of a supply-side policy?

　　A reducing welfare benefits

　　B increased population growth

　　C lower indirect taxes

　　D nationalisation of monopolies

3 'Tax receipts fell below the level of government expenditure largely due to the economy moving into recession.' What economic concept does this statement describe?

　　A structural budget deficit

　　B structural budget surplus

　　C cyclical budget deficit

　　D cyclical budget surplus

4 Which of the following is true about the national debt?

　　A The debt grows each year there is a trade deficit.

　　B As a percentage of national income, the national debt will always rise if there is a budget deficit.

　　C A fall in the national debt leads to a budget surplus.

　　D The national debt increases when there is a budget deficit.

5 Look at the diagram below.

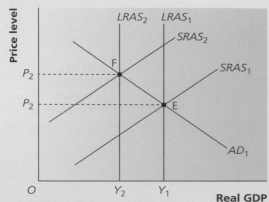

Which of the following changes would correctly explain the movement of the macroeconomic equilibrium from point E to point F?

A   a rise in productivity and a better transport network

B   a fall in the working population and higher indirect taxes

C   improved educational performance and higher wage rates

D   a fall in the cost of raw materials and increased geographical immobility

6 The first £8,000 of income earned is tax free. Any income above this level is taxed at 25%. If someone earns income in 1 year of £35,000, calculate the amount of tax they would pay.   **2 marks**

....

....

7 Income is taxed at 30% with a tax-free personal allowance of £15,000. Calculate how much income tax someone would pay if they earned an annual income of £48,000.   **2 marks**

....

....

8 Analyse how labour market reform can ease inflationary pressure in the economy.   **9 marks**

....

....

....

....

....

....

....

....

....

9 Analyse the possible causes of a budget surplus. **15 marks**

....

....

....

....

....

....

....

....

....

....

....

....

....

....

....

....

10 Analyse the reasons for government expenditure. **15 marks**

....

....

....

....

....

....

....

....

....

....

....

....

....

....

Topic 13: Data response

11 Read Extracts A, B and C and answer the following questions.   **40 marks**

60

Extract A

After 2010, the UK budget deficit became a focus for much of the government's economic policy. In particular, eliminating this deficit was seen as a priority. The government believed that reducing this deficit would restore confidence in those who would normally purchase bonds and help finance future deficits.

The cuts to government spending implemented to reduce the deficit became known as a policy of 'austerity' and many suffered hardship, as cuts were made to popular public services. The government says that lower government spending has not affected individuals as badly as others have suggested due to the significant increase in the tax-free allowances enjoyed by those working.

Many were critical of the policy of austerity and claimed that the deficit was only so large because of lower than average economic growth. Critics also claimed that cutting government spending would lead to lower growth, which would worsen the budget deficit.

Extract B

UK income tax, 2019–20

The first £12,500 of income earned is a tax-free allowance. Incomes in excess of this tax-free allowance are taxed as follows:

Income level	Tax rate
£12,500–£50,000	20%
£50,000–£150,000	40%
Over £150,000	45%

Extract C

Year	2010	2011	2012	2013	2014	2015	2016	2017	2018
Deficit (in £ billions)	147.3	122.9	136.8	94.0	98.6	79.6	57.0	37.6	32.3
Deficit (as % GDP)	9.3	7.5	8.1	5.3	5.3	4.2	2.9	1.8	1.5

Source: ONS

Government ministers now claim that austerity is over and that the government can relax spending restrictions in the economy. This is welcome news for many who have seen public services cut, as well as for those working in the public sector who have seen their incomes fall in real terms more or less continuously since 2010.

Economists are keen to encourage a wise implementation of any increase in government spending. Higher government spending would work best if used to improve the structural side of the economy, through improvements to infrastructure or education and training.

a Using Extract B, calculate the amount of income tax paid on earnings of £60,000.   **2 marks**

....

....

b Do the data contained in Extract C support the view that the government has successfully eliminated the budget deficit?   **4 marks**

....

....

....

....

c Using a diagram, analyse the impact of cuts to government spending on economic performance.   **9 marks**

....

....

....

....

....

....

....

....

....

d To what extent is the end of 'austerity' a good thing for the UK economy?   **25 marks**

Write your answer to this question on a separate sheet of paper and keep it with your workbook.

Topic 13: Essay

12 Analyse how cuts in taxation can have both demand-side and supply-side effects on the economy. **15 marks** 60

....

....

....

....

....

....

....

....

....

....

....

....

....

....

....

....

....

....

....

....

....

....

....

13 To what extent can supply-side policies help avoid conflicts and trade-offs in economic policy? **25 marks**

Write your answer to this question on a separate sheet of paper and keep it with your workbook.

Topic 14 The international economy

Globalisation

The causes and characteristics of globalisation can be examined. The consequences for less developed and also more developed countries can be studied, as well as the role of multinational corporations (MNCs) in helping with development.

Practice questions ?

AO1: Knowledge and understanding

1   Define the term 'globalisation'.   3 marks

....

....

2   What is meant by outsourcing?   3 marks

....

....

....

3   What is meant by containerisation?   3 marks

....

....

....

4   State three causes of increased globalisation.   3 marks

....

....

....

5   Explain one advantage and one disadvantage for less developed economies of attracting multinational corporations.   4 marks

....

....

....

AO2: Application

6   Explain one way in which transport innovation has contributed to globalisation.   4 marks

....

....

....

7   On an *AD/AS* diagram, show how greater investment in education and
    infrastructure can contribute to economic growth.   4 marks

AO3: Analysis

8   Explain one benefit to a less developed country of attracting multinational
    corporations (MNCs).   5 marks

....

....

....

....

....

9   Analyse how the economies of developed countries can benefit from globalisation.   9 marks

....

....

....

....

....

....

10 Analyse the drawbacks for less developed countries of increasing globalisation.   9 marks

....

....

....

....

....

....

AO4: Evaluation

Write your answers to these questions on separate sheets of paper and keep them with your workbook.

11 Assess whether MNCs are good for the economies of less developed countries. **25 marks**

12 Evaluate whether globalisation is beneficial for both developed and less developed economies. **25 marks**

Trade

The benefits of specialisation and international trade can be explained by economic models. However, many countries restrict free trade through a variety of methods, and attempt justification of this protectionism on economic grounds.

In the last 50 years, a number of trading blocs have emerged that provide free trade for members but protect their economies from trade with non-members. The UK's former membership of the EU illustrates the issues arising from this arrangement.

Practice questions ?

AO1: Knowledge and understanding

13 Define the term 'tariff'. **3 marks**

....

....

....

14 Define the term 'quota'. **3 marks**

....

....

....

15 Define the term 'customs union'. **3 marks**

....

....

....

16 What is meant by the term 'protectionism'? **3 marks**

....

....

....

17 Define the term 'absolute advantage'.   3 marks

....

....

....

18 Define the term 'comparative advantage'.   3 marks

....

....

....

19 Explain what is meant by 'export subsidies'.   3 marks

....

....

....

AO2: Application

20 Two countries are currently self-sufficient and allocate half of the factors of production to producing cars and food. The output levels in each country are as follows:

Country	Cars (units)	Food (units)
Westania	420	70
Eastopia	280	40

Show how specialisation and trade can improve on the current output position.   6 marks

Worked example

Opportunity cost of food production:

- In Westania: 1 unit of food = 6 units of cars ●————

- In Eastopia: 1 unit of food = 7 units of cars

Westania should specialise in food.

Eastopia should specialise in cars.

If each country specialises in its comparative advantage, then an improvement in output could be achieved. One possible production level would be as follows:

Country	Cars (units)	Food (units)
Westania	168	112
Eastopia	560	0

AO2: The principle of comparative advantage is that countries should specialise in products when they can produce them for a lower opportunity cost than in another country. Westania can produce food for a lower opportunity cost than Eastopia (it 'sacrifices' 6 cars for each unit of food compared with 7 cars for Eastopia). The opportunity cost of car production is lower in Eastopia — so this is what Eastopia should specialise in. Here, Westania partially specialises — it devotes 20% of its resources to cars, and 80% to food production. Overall, total output has increased (car production = 728 units, food production = 112 units).

21 Two economies are producing two different products, shown in the table below. Currently each economy is self-sufficient and devotes half of its available factors to the production of each product.

Economy	Consumer goods (units)	Capital goods (units)
Northron	80	200
Southattica	130	60
World	*210*	*260*

Calculate the total output that each country (and the world) would produce if each country specialised in its absolute advantage.   3 marks

Economy	Consumer goods (units)	Capital goods (units)
Northron	0	400
Southattica	260	0
World	*260*	*400*

....

....

22 Technolopia and Ruralia can produce computers and agricultural output. Currently neither country trades with the other and each country allocates half of its factors of production to each product. Current output is as follows:

Economy	Computers (units)	Agriculture (units)
Technolopia	480	160
Ruralia	80	80
World	*560*	*240*

Based on this data, calculate the following:

a   the opportunity cost of producing each product in each country   3 marks

....

....

....

b   the world output if each country specialised in its comparative advantage   4 marks

Economy	Computers (units)	Agricultural output (units)
Technolopia	960	0
Ruralia	0	160
World	*960*	*160*

....

....

c   a level of specialisation that guarantees world output improves on the self-sufficiency position

4 marks

Economy	Computers (units)	Agricultural output (units)
Technolopia	720	80
Ruralia	0	160
World	720	240

....

....

23 Countries A and B are currently self-sufficient and divide resources equally to produce two products. Examine the following table and explain why specialisation and trade will not be beneficial.

3 marks

Economy	Military goods (units)	Consumer goods (units)
Country A	560	320
Country B	140	80
World	700	400

....

....

....

24 Describe two changes to the pattern of UK trade with the rest of the world over the last 30 years.

4 marks

....

....

....

....

25 Draw a diagram showing the effects of a tariff being introduced in a market.

4 marks

26 State one feature of each of the following trading blocs.   3 marks

Trading bloc	Feature
Free-trade area	
Customs union	
Single market	

AO3: Analysis

27 Explain two methods of protecting an economy from imports.   6 marks

....
....
....
....
....
....

28 Analyse the benefits of international trade for a developed country.   9 marks

....
....
....
....
....
....
....
....
....
....
....
....

29 Analyse the arguments used to justify the implementation of protectionist policies.   15 marks

....

....

....

....

....

....

....

....

....

....

....

....

....

....

AO4: Evaluation

Write your answers to these questions on separate sheets of paper and keep them with your workbook.

30 To what extent is free trade beneficial for all the people of a developed economy?   25 marks

31 Evaluate the extent to which protectionism can save jobs in a high-wage economy such as the UK.   25 marks

The balance of payments

The balance of payments records the UK's financial transactions with the rest of the world. The balances on the various parts of the balance of payments are affected by many factors. Governments are concerned with imbalances on the balance of payments, although it is not always clear what the concerns are about. In the case of imbalance, governments have a variety of policies they can use to correct the balance.

Practice questions ?

AO1: Knowledge and understanding

32 Define the term 'balance of payments'.   3 marks

....

....

....

33 Define the term 'current account deficit'. *3 marks*

....

....

....

34 State the three components of the balance of payments. *3 marks*

....

....

....

35 Define the term 'primary income'. *3 marks*

....

....

....

36 Define the term 'secondary income'. *3 marks*

....

....

....

37 State three methods of correcting a trade deficit. *3 marks*

....

....

....

AO2: Application

38 Based on the following data, calculate the current account balance for this economy. *4 marks*

	£ millions
Exports of goods	165
Imports of goods	194
Exports of services	46
Imports of services	39
Primary income balance	7
Secondary income balance	(4)

....

....

....

....

39 From the following data, calculate the trade balance.   3 marks

	£ billions
Current account balance	(5.6)
Primary income balance	0.9
Secondary income balance	(0.2)

....

....

....

40 Classify each of the following transactions as either trade in goods and services, primary income or secondary income.

a   accounting services sold to foreign businesses

b   dividends received on shares in a German company

c   wages earned by a worker abroad sent back to family in a foreign country

d   television sets produced overseas but purchased in the UK

e   interest on UK bank accounts paid to overseas residents   5 marks

....

....

....

41 Classify each of the following into either factors that would increase UK exports or factors that would increase UK imports.

a   increase in UK GDP

b   faster foreign economic growth

c   increase in foreign inflation

d   reduced UK tariffs

e   increase in UK productivity   5 marks

....

....

....

AO3: Analysis

42 Explain how one supply-side policy can improve the current account balance.   5 marks

....

....

....

....

....

43 Analyse two reasons why surplus on the current account is beneficial for the UK economy.

8 marks

....

....

....

....

....

....

....

....

....

....

....

....

44 Explain how devaluation can both improve and worsen the current account balance.

8 marks

....

....

....

....

....

....

....

....

....

....

AO4: Evaluation

45 Evaluate the extent to which supply-side policies are the best way of correcting a current account imbalance.

25 marks

The worked example below shows a model conclusion from a possible response to this question. Study this closely and then attempt to answer the question fully on a separate piece of paper.

Worked example

Supply-side policies may seem to be the best way of correcting a deficit as they avoid many of the problems that other policies generate. Most of the other policies involve a trade-off or policy conflict. For example, deflationary policies conflict with the policy of low unemployment and positive economic growth. Supply-side policies are generally beneficial for all of the main economic objectives of the government and therefore it could be argued that they are the best way of correcting a current account imbalance.

> **AO4:** Very clear explanation here, outlining how supply-side policies are associated with fewer negative consequences in comparison with other methods of correcting imbalances. This is then linked back to the question posed.

Whether they are the best way would depend on how urgently the imbalance needs to be addressed. Supply-side policies are generally long-term policies and the effects of their implementation would take some time (perhaps years) to improve the current account balance. This means that if the imbalance needs to be corrected quickly, then supply-side policies would perhaps not be the best approach.

> **AO4:** Good point raised here, in considering the urgency of the problem and the timescale needed for the solution to work as an important issue.

In economics we often look for solutions that have the lowest opportunity cost as the best way of allocating resources. In this case, given the reduced number of policy conflicts with other objectives, supply-side policies would be the best approach to pursue.

> **AO4:** A good link here with the point that economics is about allocating resources in the best possible manner. This is then linked back to the title of the question and it is good to end with an overall recommendation.

46 The UK has maintained a deficit on its current account for many years. To what extent is this sustainable?

25 marks

Write your answer to this question on a separate sheet of paper and keep it with your workbook.

Exchange rate systems

The exchange rate is determined by a number of factors. Governments can choose to allow the exchange rate to float freely or can intervene to either manage or fix the exchange rate. There is a further case to be assessed about whether to join a currency union such as the eurozone.

AO1: Knowledge and understanding

47 Define the term 'floating exchange rate'. 3 marks

> **Worked example**
>
> A floating exchange rate is where the actual value of the currency is determined by market forces of demand and supply, with no attempt by the government to influence its value.

AO1: Incorporates all that is needed to define fully the term 'floating exchange rate': both what the exchange rate means (value of currency determined by market forces) and what is meant by the 'floating' aspect (no government intervention).

48 Define the term 'fixed exchange rate'. 3 marks

49 What is meant by a managed exchange rate? 3 marks

50 Explain the term 'open market operations' in the context of exchange rate management. 3 marks

51 What is meant by a currency union? 3 marks

AO2: Application

52 If £1 = €1.25 and £1 = $1.50, calculate the price of €1 in terms of US dollars ($). 2 marks

53 Income per capita in Germany is €57,000 and income per capita in the USA is $62,000. The current exchange rate is £1 = $1.20 and £1 = €1.10. Calculate income per capita expressed in pounds (£s) for both Germany and the USA, to the nearest pound, and state who has the highest income per capita (in £s). 3 marks

54 Construct an exchange rate diagram for the pound (£), showing a rise in UK imports. **4 marks**

55 Classify each of the following factors into either those that would increase or those that would decrease the exchange rate.

a   increase in UK imports

b   increase in foreign GDP

c   increase in UK's relative productivity

d   increase in inward foreign direct investment (FDI)

e   increase in speculation that UK interest rates will fall   **5 marks**

AO3: Analysis

56 Analyse, using an appropriate diagram, one reason why the exchange rate would rise.   **6 marks**

Worked example

One reason would be a rise in relative interest rates. This is where UK interest rates rise in relation to interest rates in other economies. This will make the return on UK financial assets more attractive, which will attract an inflow of hot money into the UK. As a result, there will be an increase in the demand for sterling. This is shown on the following diagram as a rightwards shift in the demand (for sterling) curve (from D_1 to D_2). The value of the currency will rise from €1.30 to €1.40.

AO1: Clear reason identified — rise in relative interest rates.

AO2: A nicely developed logical chain of reasoning — notice how each successive part of the argument builds on the earlier part.

AO3: Further development and a good link to a correct and fully labelled diagram.

57 Analyse one benefit and one drawback of allowing the exchange rate to float. **8 marks**

....

....

....

....

....

....

....

....

AO4: Evaluation

Write your answers to these questions on separate sheets of paper and keep them with your workbook.

58 To what extent was the UK government correct in not joining the euro currency union? **25 marks**

59 Evaluate the extent to which a floating exchange rate is the best exchange rate policy available. **25 marks**

Economic growth and development

Economic growth and development are connected but are distinct. Less developed economies have common characteristics, and various indicators are used to measure their development, such as the human development index (HDI). A variety of factors help in both economic growth and development, but there are other factors that act as barriers to growth and development. Certain economic policies help an economy to grow and to develop, and aid and trade help in promoting both of these aspects.

Practice questions ?

AO1: Knowledge and understanding

60 Distinguish between economic growth and economic development. **2 marks**

....

....

....

61 State the three indicators used to calculate the HDI. **3 marks**

....

....

....

62 State four common features of a less developed economy.　　4 marks

....

....

....

....

63 Explain what is meant by a 'market-based strategy' for promoting growth and development.　　3 marks

....

....

....

AO2: Application

64 In the context of attaining development, classify each of the following into either market-based or interventionist strategies.　　6 marks

Removing maximum prices	Trade liberalisation
Debt cancellation	Policies to attract FDI
Overseas aid	Increases in state welfare

....

....

....

....

65 In the context of attaining development, classify each of the following into either market-based or interventionist strategies.　　6 marks

Tariff removal	Decreased subsidies
Investment in education	Construction of transport network
Privatisation of state-owned businesses	Policies to maximise aid

....

....

....

....

66 Explain one way in which over-reliance on primary products can be a barrier to development.　　4 marks

....

....

....

AO3: Analysis

67 Explain two ways in which state investment can help an economy reach developed status.

6 marks

....

....

....

....

....

68 Analyse how poorly developed infrastructure may prevent development being attained.   6 marks

....

....

....

....

....

....

69 Analyse the policies that a less developed country can use to move closer to reaching development.

9 marks

....

....

....

....

....

....

....

....

AO4: Evaluation

70 To what extent is an increase in trade the best method for a country to reach developed country status?

25 marks

Write your answer to this question on a separate sheet of paper and keep it with your workbook.

Topic 14: Multiple choice and short answer

1   In the UK, the exchange rate appreciates from £1 = €1.10 to £1 = €1.30. What is the most likely effect of this change in the currency's value?

   A   UK imports from countries using the euro (€) will become more expensive.

   B   UK exports to countries using the euro will increase in volume.

   C   UK exports to countries using the euro will increase in value.

   D   UK imports from countries using the euro will become cheaper.

2   Which of the following would contribute to an inflow on the primary income balance of the balance of payments in an economy?

   A   donations made from the UK to overseas countries

   B   sales of financial services provided by UK companies

   C   dividends earned by UK residents on shares in a Germany company

   D   foreign direct investment into the UK

3   Which of the following would normally lead to a fall in the UK's exchange rate?

   A   a rise in UK exports

   B   a rise in UK imports

   C   a rise in UK interest rates

   D   a fall in foreign interest rates

4   Which of the following is not an appropriate method for reducing the volume of imports?

   A   tariffs

   B   deflationary policies

   C   supply-side policies

   D   revaluation of exchange rate

5   In which of the following scenarios would a devaluation of the currency improve the current account balance?

	Price elasticity of demand for exports	Price elasticity of demand for imports
A	−0.40	−0.60
B	−0.70	−0.25
C	−0.30	−0.70
D	−0.05	−1.00

6   The pound sterling (£) has risen by 10% against the US dollar ($) over the last year to £1 = $1.35. Calculate the value of $1 in terms of pounds 1 year ago.   **2 marks**

7 The table below shows the value of a country's currency against other currencies, in index number form.

Year	Exchange rate index (2018 = 100)
2017	106
2018	100
2019	97
2020	96

Calculate the percentage change in the exchange rate index between 2017 and 2020.   **2 marks**

....

....

8 From the following data, calculate the trade balance for the economy.   **2 marks**

Current account data	£ millions
Exports of goods	811,212
Imports of goods	787,979
Exports of services	231,241
Imports of services	98,010

....

....

9 Explain, using a diagram, how a government can reduce the level of imports into an economy.   **9 marks**

....

....

....

....

....

....

10 Analyse, using a numerical example or diagram, how comparative advantage can allow all economies to be better off.   **15 marks**

....

....

....

....

....

....

....

....

....

....

Exam-style questions

Topic 14: Data response

11 Read Extracts A, B and C and answer the following questions.   **50 marks**

Extract A

In 2014, the current account deficit reached 5.5% of GDP, which was the largest deficit since records began in 1948. However, some economists claim that the large deficit does not matter. Even if other areas of the balance of payments show deficits, the UK can borrow money to cover the deficit. If the exchange rate is allowed to float, then the currency can fall in value and exports would be boosted.

Extract B

Other economists are concerned about the large current account deficit. This is because it is blamed on declining performance of UK exports. Even with a fall in the value of the currency in recent years, there is still a growing deficit on foreign trade. Others have warned that if the deficit grows in size or remains for a prolonged period, then investors will begin to become nervous and will be less willing to fund the current account deficit by placing money into the UK. This may force interest rates higher to prevent an outflow of 'hot money'.

Extract C

UK economic growth and current account balance, 2010–18

Year	GDP growth per year (%)	Current account balance (£ millions)
2010	1.7	−53,620
2011	1.6	−32,206
2012	1.4	−63,842
2013	2.0	−90,692
2014	2.9	−90,897
2015	2.3	−93,165
2016	1.8	−102,790
2017	1.8	−68,365
2018	1.4	−81,644

a Using Extracts A and C, calculate the size of UK GDP in 2014.   **2 marks**

....

....

b Do the data in Extract C support the existence of an inverse relationship
between GDP growth and the current account balance?   **4 marks**

....

....

....

....

c Analyse how supply-side policies can eliminate a current account deficit.   **9 marks**

....

....

....

....

....

....

....

....

....

d To what extent does it matter that the UK has a large current account deficit? **25 marks**
*Write your answer to this question on a separate sheet of paper and keep it
with your workbook.*

Topic 14: Essay

12 Analyse the factors that would cause an increase in the deficit on the current account.

15 marks **60**

....

....

....

....

....

....

....

....

....

....

....

....

....

....

....

....

....

....

....

....

....

....

....

13 To what extent is devaluation of a currency good for an economy?   **25 marks**

Write your answer to this question on a separate sheet of paper and keep it with your workbook.